Auscultation

T0164117

For Dan and Nick
my two suns

Auscultation

Ilse Pedler

Seren is the book imprint of
Poetry Wales Press Ltd.
Suite 6, 4 Derwen Road, Bridgend, Wales, CF31 1LH
www.serenbooks.com
facebook.com/SerenBooks
twitter@SerenBooks

The right of Ilse Pedler to be identified as
the author of this work has been asserted in accordance
with the Copyright, Designs and Patents Act, 1988.

© Ilse Pedler, 2021.

ISBN: 978-1-78172-626-6
ebook: 978-1-78172-627-3

A CIP record for this title is available from the British Library.

The publisher acknowledges the financial assistance of the Books Council of Wales.

Cover artwork: © RunPhoto, Getty Images.

Printed in Bembo by Severn, Gloucester.

Contents

★

auscultation *n*

1. The act of listening.
2. Medicine – The act of listening for sounds made by internal organs, as the heart and lungs, to aid in the diagnosis of certain disorders.

Visit to the Vets

I'm listening when I say *how are you today?*
I'm listening when I tilt my head just so.
I'm listening when I say hello to Fluffy, Sooty or Rex.
I'm listening when Rex pees up the door.
I'm listening when you get a text and text back.
I'm listening when you let your kids climb on the table.
I'm listening when you answer your phone say, *I'm in the vets, I can't talk.*
I'm listening when you carry on talking.
I'm listening when you say *I can't put my finger on what's wrong.*
I'm listening when you say *but I know he's just not right.*
I'm listening when you say you've looked it up on the internet.
I'm listening when you say *are you sure?*
I'm listening when you ask me to predict the future.
I'm listening when he growls and you say *don't worry, he won't bite you.*
I'm listening when he tries to bite me.
I'm listening when you ask me what's wrong and I've already told you.
I'm listening when you start telling me about your other dog.
I'm listening when I've heard the same thing five times already.
I'm listening when I plug my ears with the stethoscope.
I'm listening when you say *your job must be so interesting.*
I'm listening when you say *you vets are all rip off merchants.*
I'm listening when you snap at your partner.
I'm listening when your kids go quiet and hold hands.
I'm listening to the sound of your self-importance filling the room.
I'm listening as your opinions start polishing their firearms.
I'm listening to the emptiness of your wallet in the silence.
I'm listening as your dead husband stands behind you putting
        his overcoat around your shoulders.

Teach Me To Kill

Sit me down on a wooden bench
and let me hear the scream
of chalk on blackboard.

Draw me diagrams and flow charts,
give me a slate and pencil
and instruct me how to scratch them out.

Give me homework;
printouts and worksheets
that I can strike through with my coloured pens.

Indicate the important bits,
the bits I'll be tested on at the end of term
in the multiple-choice question paper

along with my fellow students;
the hangmen, the slaughter men,
the ones who draw up lethal injections

who strap people to gurneys,
sit in the chair to test the restraints,
the ones with the electric paddles or captive bolt

and the ones who hover in the doorway
who aren't officially here, who just turn up the drip.
They won't be taking the exam.

You won't find this course in any prospectus
or other promotional material
it is advertised by word of mouth.

Teach me to kill in the smallest lecture theatre
with the unmarked door. Teach me the tricks
of the trade, how to kill and then carry on.

Every Time a Performance

Through the wire-gridded windows
of the heavy double doors
a table – centre stage – metal stalked.

Above
the bright bowl of a theatre light
looking on with its own astonished eyes.

We emerge – stage left – like ghosts
in our pale green gowns
bowed at the back

stretching translucent gloves over scrubbed hands
snapping them down on cuffed wrists,
we take our positions – wait for the cue.

Silence is the stave we work from,
listening for the steadying intro
of the two-time base line

we begin to dot the melody
in curtly commanded syllables.
Palms are offered

transactions occur,
blood beads urgently
from the lines we draw.

Surgical Instruments

Line them up;
Backhaus towel clips,
Allis tissue forceps,
Mayo scissors curved and straight,
a Volkman scoop, Kerrison rongeurs,
Lanes, Treves and Adson Brown
solving the problems
of the soft persistence of tissue.

★

Tools to clamp and grasp, to retract
muscle until you see the white strain
of fibres, to probe and dilate,
to ratchet back bone, exposing cavities,

cavities that are not still – a moment
and flesh bulges around the shanks of metal,
blood pools and glistens, organs slide
to evade capture by finely serrated jaws.

★

Heron-necked cheatles pause
over the silver fish of instruments,
plunge to skim them off one by one
from the green lake of the drape.

Mosquito forceps, their fine tips
sipping the surface, rat tooth forceps
nipping the skin with their mean
little mouths - crocodile forceps

Miss Freak's Whelping Forceps

Wrapped in cloth in a Gladstone bag
boiled in second best saucepans, now here,
laid out on velvet in this museum case;
delicate, slim shanked, small angled loops to cup
the head and ease it through.

Mr Hobday's at the front,
the pioneer with his rigid rings of steel
to clamp the foetal skull, McLean
with longer shafts for deeper access,
Elliot with thicker loops for crushing action.

How they laboured, these men
with their unforgiving fists of metal
but in the feral hours where instinct loosens
itself from shadows, it's Miss Freaks we reach for
to coax the unborn to crown the light.

The Calving

Straw hastily spread
crisps under the frost's force,
a single dusty bulb
explores the darkness.

She stamps a warning,
twists her tethered head,
the whites of her eyes
moons of fear.

The cowman and his lad
stamp their numbing toes,
thick square hands
freezing on the halter's buckle.

I prepare ropes and a jack,
roll up my sleeves,
take off my watch and ring,
push them deep into my pocket.

I trail cold gel up my arm
like the track of a snail,
pinch my fingers together to ease
the passage and slip inside.

Following the wall of the womb
I touch nose and ear,
inch loops of rope
over knuckles of hooves,

twist the ends over the hooks
on the jack and start to pull.
She bellows her pain,
crushes my bones on hers.

We both strain to birth
this new life – and only she
and I are warm,
and I am at the warmth's core.

Neighbours

Allocation is the simplest option,
sows batched according to insemination date

then the wait; three months, three weeks,
three days until the farrowing house,

its rows of metal crates, power-washed walls
faint tang of swimming pools. Heaving

neighbours divided by two metre lengths
in tune only to the song of hormones

the tipping point into contraction,
until crate after crate becomes quiet

and the whole house sways to the rhythm of birth.
Delivery after delivery of slimy pink,

flapping forward slicked-back ears
trembling towards the teat on autopilot.

When the door opens, a sow barks a warning, triggers
the discordant peal of metal bars; flies rise in a layer.

Piglets dispossessed of teats scatter,
duck into the creep and the safety of the lamp.

Three weeks and another moving day,
sows weaned in batches to the service pen,

nose pressing on nose to rediscover each other,
check who's missing, who'll carry on to the next round.

The Importance of Air

Late afternoon when the low sun casts long
shadows on the field, the herd makes its way in order
to the collecting yard. The stockman slides the heavy
doors of the milking parlour open and then is gone
into the disinfected gloom. The first cow
shoulders her way in, eager to give up her milk

from her vulgar blue-veined udder. Dribbles of milk
are lost unnoticed from those waiting and form long
meandering creeks on the shit-splashed concrete. Each cow
a collection of monumental bones in a predetermined order
covered over with stretched hide. All softness gone
into the swollen bag they haul around waiting for the heavy

snatch of the cluster, each sucking rubber sleeve heavy
on the teat. Each udder drained and the white froth of milk
measured and emptied into the bulk tank and once she's gone
another takes her place quickly from the long
queue outside the parlour, never varying the order.
The stockman checks the ear tags, each cow

a number and in the office, each number, a cow's
worth of statistics and a coloured pin on the heavy
circular chart on the office wall. Every colour an order;
red for service, blue for calving, green to dry off the milk.
She shifts restlessly about the calving pen, her long
wait almost over. The yard is empty, the others long gone

back up to the field, the gate closed and the stockman gone
to clean the parlour. Her belly tightens and the cow
feels the first pains, she's been waiting for this all day long.
She finds a corner in the calving pen and lays down, her belly heavy
with pressing calf, and her udder filling with the first thick milk.
She bellows through the pain; she knows there is an order

to these things. The stockman stops and listens, orders
his dog to stay and joins her in the calving pen, gone
is any thought of home. At last comes the gush of bloody fluid and milk

and the gasping rush of calf, huge and seal-like in its sac. The cow licks with her long sure tongue and the calf lifts its head, heavy with the importance of air. The cow breathes in calf all night long.

In the morning, the stockman gives the order to hold the cow and before she can turn, the calf is gone. Her udder swells, heavy with milk but he'll be back to take her to the parlour before long.

Castrating Calves

Golden Shovel after William Carlos Williams

One by one the sweet-breathed calves – so
innocent – are held as much
as is needed, which depends
on the sharpness of her knife upon
their soft hairless pouches of skin. A
practised cut releases the slippery warmth, a pull and twist and red
tailed they are tossed to land with the rest of the catch in the wheel
barrow
silver glazed
pulsating with
the last of their lives, while out in the rain,
quick-eyed workhouse collies – water
beading the mats of their coats – know to stay beside
her ready to snatch at the mouthfuls of freed flesh. The
woman straightens and with a flick of her white
thin wrist throws the last of them to the chickens.

Grunting Up*

Who would have thought that these great slab-sided beasts
who fall to their knees and slump belly up,
would sing this rhythmic grunting lullaby?

Weight drops from back and loins but
swollen undulating glands seem added on,
like a full frill at the bottom of a skirt.

The piglets rush to their particular nipple
and plug on, tongues curling, eyes closed,
chubby fingers, lined up, reaching.

And then she begins. This low throbbing,
this song to the milk flow,
this crooning hymn.

* *"Grunting up" is the name given to the noise
a sow makes when her piglets are sucking.*

Breed Standard

Tenacious, hard-working sheep dog, of great tractability
from the Kennel Club of Great Britain Breed Standards

Fine-tuned to catch
  each twitch
of the hand,
   each whispered
command,
 the collie;
sleek-backed
rigid,
trammelled
tight to leg,
pitched high
   as an e string
over-wound.

While in the bright distance,
the fells unfold –
beckon –
a skylark rises
unchains its throat.

Ploughing

Modern tractors have GPS steering systems so the driver doesn't have to turn around to see where he has ploughed. There are also work lights which turn on when it gets dark so the farmer can plough at night. If the weather turns hot there is air conditioning. Ploughing was an art; judging the point to turn at the end of the field and lift the plough took time and patience to learn; turn too quickly and the edges of the field are unused which reduces yields, turn too slowly and the lifted plough may get caught in trees and prevent the turn altogether.

One farmer I know can plough all day and night, he says he turns his mind off and considers the importance of other things. I've seen him turn the earth into brown waves then watch the gulls dive for fish, wheel and turn somersaults in great clouds. I have seen him catch onto mare's tails and turn them into the wind to gallop. One day he carried on at the edge, forgot to turn and followed the sky up. There he is now, creel caught in a net of stars turning and turning on the Earth's rim.

Shearing Sheds

after Gerard Benson

Sometimes I think about the shearing sheds
and the bowed backs of men
sleeves rolled up
wrists slick with sweat
and the sweet smell of shit
and the surprised faces of sheep
slit amber eyes wide,
turned on their backs
rolled from side to side
knuckled legs skywards
and I think about the shouts
for the next and the swearing
and the scorched smoulder of roll-ups
and most of all I think about
the grumble of clippers revving
over skin, peeling back grey fleeces
to release bony bleached bodies
that stumble off
too dazed to make a noise,
to the release pen where they stare
at each other in astonishment.

A Smaller Man

He was a smaller man when I saw him again,
his clothes one size too big,
his face, a pencil sketch
of the original.

He was pulling up old pea plants,
desiccated pods,
twisted and split
spilling out wrinkled peas.

How are you coping?
We're OK, things take longer.
It's amazing the time you waste
in a supermarket. I had no idea.

I remember him throwing a straw bale over
his shoulder like a baby,
catching and upending a ewe
in one vast sweep.

He looked down, and the sound of his sigh
was like a puncture in a tractor tyre.
He twisted a pea stalk round and around
his finger, then let it drop

and we watched as the wind lifted it
as though it were nothing and carried
it on puppet strings across the garden
until it was gone.

Rowan Points to its Treasure

Solitary on the high fells,
back bent against the gale's blast
muscles knotted under bark,
cables of tendons twisting
on an anchor of wiry toes gripping
through the crust of soil
into cracks of rock.

In days that become black and white,
when crags like burnt cinder toffee
crown through a scream of snow,
it stretches a fingerpost of branches
splintered by the bite
of ice and wind

signalling a hope to its cave of roots
a hollow in the storm's howl,
a treasure hoard
barely visible,
the wisps of wool.

From Darkness

From this pitchy void we are required
to extract our meaning.

But what flickering moment
defines our existence?

What sets the electrons spinning
around a kernel of identity

in this endless succession of small bangs?
Unique collections of atomic specks

we strive to stabilise our meandering orbits,
insert cross links in a vast polymerisation.

Shuffle the hand, tiny fragments of protein
map out another version.

Don't drop the cards,
one slip changes everything.

CaCO$_3$

Limestone, marble, chalk or this spiralled
skeleton, spun in crystal sheets, pearl lids

covering the softest insecurities and from
these mineral beginnings, a form

of delicate complexity surprises itself
but unseen, its beauty is harled, is left

concealed in crevices, its journey coursed
from pulling silent undertow to scoured

by grit and tide, unfurrowed and littering
the shore. We seize the pearly glitter in

our hands; each one a death, each one a united
purpose finished. It begins again – the bonds untied.

Chiropractic

Shell prised open
white flesh exposed,
I am a sea creature.

Cool hands stroke
the back I never see
as I am unhooked

I ebb and flow
against the tide
of her.

I become the shore,
waves tap and smack
along my waterline,

nuggets of bone,
their spiny processes
tilt and groan

to her touch –
tiny adjustments
in the current's drag,

released nerves sigh,
I am aligned
in the receding water.

The Hill Ewe's Pasture

She returns each year, the whisper of stones
in her bones, the wind her breath and the curve
of the fells her helix, ridges preserved
in her eye spiralling away, all of
her vision imprinted by what she knows
and is part of. She is hefted to this
mountainside, passing the knowledge on through
umbilical cord and thick milk, mother
to daughter to daughter – home. But when I
return, the lines between us are redrawn
and familiar boundaries defended
in our unforgiving pasture. I can
only turn my back to the flattening
rain and search for shelter in the hollows.

Unmade

I come from a place where children were seen and not heard,
where mantelpiece clocks chimed the quarter hours
and lavender bags hung like seed pods in wardrobes.

I come from a place where vegetables were dug from the garden
and left by the back door for tea,
where trouser pockets were treasure troves of string and Polo mints
and a *nice piece of brown bread and butter* was a show of affection.
I come from a place of antimacassars.

I come from a place of coral lipstick,
where diet sheets were stuck on fridge doors
and eyebrows were drawn on in pencil each morning.

I come from a place where perfumes were sprayed on like shellac,
where firm-control body shapers dried like shrivelled cocoons on the line
and hostess trollies held court in lounges.
I come from a place of quiet men.

I come from a place where people were *as common as muck,*
where the dining room table was polished to a mirror shine
and we ate our meals from trays on our knees in silence.

I come from a place where I was always *too young to have an opinion,*
where one parent would sleep on the sofa for days
and shattered glass would be swept up quietly with a dustpan and brush.

I come from a place where I tried to be noticed by becoming less,
where eventually there was so little of me, I slipped out
through the crack between the door and frame
and nobody noticed I was gone.

Heirloom

Inside my mother's sewing box, little plaits
of embroidery silks lie in ordered rainbows.

Most evenings she licks the end
of a strand into a point and threads it through

my eye with fierce concentration, fixing
me in little stitches to the stretched canvas.

My scalp smarts as she tugs
the tangles out of my hair and anchors

it in neat bunches. My neck itches
with the stiff collar of the dress she chain

stitches for me and my toes are pinched
by the tight black shoes buttoned with French knots.

In running stitch, she outlines a straight-backed
chair for me to sit on and a book for my hands.

Finally, with little split stitches she carefully stabs
out a smile on my face.

A Bag of Lemons

He was a square of a man; shoulders filling the door frame,
belly broad, feet set apart, steady against the yaw
and sway of the planks as he worked his days
on the promise of the sea.

He took the Docker's cut; a box of oranges like golden suns,
a side of lamb, the bottles of rum. If his horse came in he'd put
half the winnings behind the clock on the mantelpiece
and drink the rest away.

You were his daughter; the first in the family at the Grammar,
better than them in your uniform and shiny shoes,
then your mother died and you were left on your own
with the little ones and the baby.

You darned your dreams into the holes of their socks, turned
sheets sides to middle and flattened them in the mangle.
One day he brought home a bag of lemons,
you cut the perfumed skin and took a bite,
carried the bitterness with you for all your years.

Following the Motorways

There were always maps.
Dog-eared rows on the bookcase,
framed prints on the wall,
and the weighty red atlas
by the side of the armchair,
each night a different country.

You would sit for hours studying
A-roads and mountain ranges;
you welcomed the new motorways,
straight blue lines
leading in one direction only,
National Service – university – work.

Time was neatly divided:
climbing holidays in the Alps,
a season ticket to the Hallé,
politics and beer
in the back room of The George,
and your girlfriend.

It caught you out,
the sixth-month pregnancy,
no road through that one.
So you did the honourable thing,
then changed jobs, moved to a small town
in the Midlands, just off the M5.

I remember you in the evenings
your thumb fitting perfectly
in the worn spot on the atlas cover,
retracing old routes
trying to fix the shifting borders.

The Thief

It was only by elimination that we recognised you;
reduced, folded into the starched envelope of sheets,
we were afraid to wake you. Were you asleep
or just lulled by the birdsong of hums and beeps?

We were intimidated by the machinery of illness,
tubes disappearing under covers, lake smooth and white,
only your right arm heavy on the surface and the deep bruise
spreading around the catheter, the little crust of blood.

Visitors to other beds laughed, brought gifts of news,
asked questions, understood the whispered answers.
We could only sit mesmerised by your heart fluttering
against its bark-stripped basket of ribs.

Back home, we watched a magpie bobbing and waiting
on the garage roof, its head cocked at the high notes
in the hedge; a blackbird's nest, the parents desperately
trying noisy distractions, flying out of different exits.

Suspended in the familiarity of waiting, we could only
let our eyes drift from the window to our cups of tea,
and inevitably, with the steel forceps of its beak
the magpie seized a fledgling from the nest.

Frantically, the parents threw themselves into dive after dive,
a frenzy of raucous screaming cracking their voices,
as they recklessly battered the thief with their wings,
small fists beating against your chest.

The silence is

never silent

our bodies are   never silent.

Listen.

Can you hear the heart's relentless throbbing
    muscling blood through valves
        gulping like fish mouths
           on the surface of the water?

Today the silence is   waiting

here in this funeral parlour   with its rose-scented air fresheners
that are making me feel sick   but I can't go outside

I must sit still and silent next to my mother
    who is still and silent enough for both of us
        as we listen to our blood inching uphill

back to our hearts   one pulse at a time.

Then in the undertaker's office   where the silence is

lost for words at the size of him,
    the rolls of jowls that wobble as he talks about
        high-gloss finishes and solid brass handles
           and all I can think of is   who will carry him?

I ask. *What about cardboard?*

The silence is   awkward

he sucks in air through flared nostrils
    whistles it around scrolled passageways
        hisses it out with the words

most people want the best for their loved ones

and I should have got up then
and taken my mother by the arm and walked away

but he reaches under his desk and pulls out an urn
    and as he's talking, he's twisting the top
        and it comes apart with a sucking

WHOP

The silence is   shocked

our breath softens to a whisper in the sponge of our lungs
        and my mother lets out a little muffled sob
            like a dog being kicked.

The silence is   embarrassed

then it gets angry   and I stand up   and we need to get out

right now

but we know that somewhere cold
        the reason we're here   is lying   waiting
            and the stethoscope's ruled that

his silence is   final

and all that noise

                                        had to stop.

Auscultation

Tick tock   non stop
footstep   raindrop
roof top   drum beat
birds' feet   moth wing
stretched skin   tattoo
tail wag   wooden floor
closing door   lip smacking
slapping shut
but
softly   distant
ly.
Repeat
rock drip   slip slop
choppiness   undercurrent
groynes   break   water
corpuscles spurt and froth against the jut and not quite stop
of slosh and swell and wash and
eddy   and
murmur
it
whisper
it
butterfly
butterfly
butter
fly
but

Voicemail

I need you to be there
    to allow the
        necessity
            of this knowledge
                to pass from me,
                    to where it is
anticipated.

I need to hear your ear
    fidget
against the cool smooth
of the phone
then make a seal
so no words
    can leak
out.

I need to picture your lips
gripping tightly
on a breath
then opening slowly
    as you ask me questions.

There will be
            questions.

I need you to be there,
so I don't have to speak
    after a beep
and leave words like
    diagnosis
and
    prognosis
        hanging

Lessons Learnt

I never forgot you telling me my surgery
wasn't bad for a woman.
I never forgot the letter of apology you made me write
for the mistake you caused.
I never forgot you saying you were sick of my baby
before he was even born.

Now I see you in the neat lines of my sutures,
feel you in the quick confidence of my scalpel,
hear your voice when I tell my students
to be *bold, bloody and resolute*

but I couldn't sign your retirement book.

All this accumulation of knowledge

how to duck under barbed wire without breaking stride
which end of a gate to climb over
a familiarity with latches

when to use a gypsy twitch to calm a fractious mare
the safest place to stand behind a cow
the knots farmers tie in baler twine

which calf needs to curl its rough tongue
around your fingers to learn to drink from a bucket
the ferocity of mothers

where to find the sweet spot behind an old boar's ear
and by scratching it – bring him to his knees
the gauges of needles

the voice to use to soothe a fearful dog
an acquaintance with the silences of cats
the irregularities of heartbeats

whether skin can be coaxed and anchored over gaps
the balance of a scalpel between fingers
the different colours of blood

why looking away is sometimes the best option
how life leaves through the backs of eyes
when to tighten a grip – when to let go.

Roadblock

The night is a vast blank letter waiting
to be written and suddenly here are the words:

blue and red interrupting the darkness
glancing off shocked faces,

hi-vis jackets, shoulders hunched
against bad news, stationary cars.

I lower my window, say I am the vet
and am waved on through.

In the road a horse, spotlit, head down,
resting a leg as though tired from a ride,

no blood, just trembling under my hands,
steam beading the fine hairs on its flared nostrils,

and that leg; it is like a child's drawing,
bones angled all the wrong way.

I don't have what I need and am taken
to the surgery, speed elongating

the streetlights, then back past journeys
put on hold, through the roadblock

to the horse and its bent back leg,
sweat starting to carve rivers in his coat, his heat

and the pulse of him that I can feel still
through the rigid cold of the gun.

Cabinet of Curiosities

Hearts unticking
stopped clocks,

a horse's jawbone
        corrugated molars
furrowed brown,

a bezoar,
a bladder stone,

a tibia stripped of flesh
the malignant trabeculae
crumbling to dust,

a flea circus,
            see the trapeze springing
their shrimpy bodies from bar to bar

and in the corners
        the eyes
too many to count,

and I'm the last pattern fired
on their fading retinas

or perhaps not
            but they cannot report back,

sometimes when I pass
I hear them rattling to get out.

Wildlife

This time a rescued owl
at the bottom of the cardboard box.

I secure its legs
surprised
by the spare
tautness,
the tufted
articulations
of bone,
the softness
of feathers
cloaking
scalpel sharp
stilettos.
I examine
wings for wounds,
assess
emaciation,
look up
to see I am fixed
by unsounded
circles
of black.

I offer it the refuge of a cage,
with a warning click
it turns its back.

Snipe of the Woods

Earthbound, leaf hidden
bird of the long migration

who, when Baltic ice locks tight
reads the script, slips

into graphite sky
over snow and snow

west blown,
who jibs and dips

over St Peter's spires
cloud crowned

belly light
sea bound.

A night scribe flown
into a grey town,

the search for woods
that hide in mirror towers

reflects too late,
a feather shroud,

scribbled life unwound,
we gather round

and wonder why it missed
what was in front of it.

From space – a burning heart

the bright capsule of motorway
pierced by filaments of light
reaching to outposts.

Grey arteries radiate from its tangled core,
veins of sluggish water
a thrombus of plastic and leaves.

It hypertrophies
in angular folds of concrete
layered over bones,

domes of churches corseted
between sheets of glass and steel,
the curve of its ankle.

Underground a writhing
wormery of tunnels and cables.

Its pitted integument, keloid scarred,
thrown into strata;

the dust of ash and embers,
the crust of excrement from cattle driven over cobbles,
the trunks of London Planes stained black with shrapnel.

And all those hearts,
beating through tower blocks and offices
pulses thrumming through streets, under pavements.

Disturbance is standing still,
resisting the motion.

Behind City Doors

The city steals sleep, the city hides lives,
people step out of themselves into shadows.
A face in the crowd becomes lost
in the crowd of faces, no one meets your eyes.

People step out of themselves into shadows
the shadows walk about unnoticed.
In the crowd of faces no one meets your eyes,
tuned out, looking down is the safest way home.

The shadows walk about unnoticed
the streets are never empty,
tuned out, looking down is the safest way home
yet all our front doors look the same.

The streets are never empty –
glimpses of lives on high-rise balconies
yet all our front doors look the same,
just wood concealing secrets.

Glimpses of lives on high-rise balconies,
a face in the crowd becomes lost
behind wood concealing secrets.
The city steals sleep, the city hides lives.

Meditations

Under fallen logs the busiest habitats occur,
the dark surges with industrious connections,
of which we hear nothing as we pass;
food chains begin in silence.

★

Can the thought of a mountain be as hard to climb?
The struggle for height, eyes on the horizon,
while sheep tread their connecting paths to shelter,
the best grass and look up, rarely.

★

A house with no doors shows us an honesty
or maybe thoughts too complex to fill the gaps,
we tack up sheets in the frames
while we contemplate separation.

★

Skyscrapers sway in high winds
to a rhythm of breathing.
In Beijing, people talk of particulate matter
and put on masks as well as shoes when leaving home.

★

I watch from the edge of landfill
and see the patch that is you being picked over.
I want them to pause, seize something, stow
it greedily in a dirty bag and cradle it home.

I want them to turn it out onto a table,
hold it up to the light, polish it with a soft cloth.

The Young Man and the Fox

The fox waited by the side of the road
headlights making mirrors of its eyes.
Its nose a nugget of wet coal
mined from the strata of scents:
pepper of crushed leaves
stale musk of badger
the clean heaviness of turned earth.
Now it was suffocating
in the seam of man.

After his parents left,
the young man listened
to the drone of cars cage the room,
the window judder with a passing bus.
He put clothes on hangers,
arranged his books,
cradled in his hands
the wooden bowl and photo frame
his girlfriend had made.

He ripped Blu Tack into balls
and fixed himself to the wall
in photos, ticket stubs
and more photos.
Scraping from the dustbins made him turn
to the window and in the moonlit
lamps of the fox's eyes
he saw fields and hedgerows
and the silver wind of the lane home.
With a russet spill of its tail
the fox turned.

Lines of Communication

Wires thread telegraph poles
loose stitches on the high moor,

birds dip and arrow away from their young – hearts
tight knots of muscle on the skim of the wind.

It used to be that I could feel the tug of you,
knew that you were on the end of a line

in a friend's house, or a phone box
its floor littered with cigarette stubs.

Now your voice, when it comes, wheels
in from top floor flats or late-night chicken shops,

breaks on the thudding rollers of a basement disco
or the whispered breath of, *I'm in the library.*

Today the bird thinking danger is over
returns to her nest and finds it empty.

Love Song

We are connected by flattened grey umbilical cords, rolling out for miles. Spanned by steel and concrete in heroic symmetry, punctuated by graceful stalks of light, the only decisions determined by numbers. North is straight ahead I am geographically reassured. London is never far away and there is always a trainer in the central reservation. The logistics of separation solved by wheels and refrigeration. A willow man runs away arms outstretched, an angel observes magnificently. A voice tells me to continue until further notice.

The Queen Bee

I'd been wanting to tell you all weekend;
glanced at you now, son draped across your knees
saying *Daddy look*, at some small thing
and you looked and pushed his blond hair
out of his eyes, two heads bent together.

I'd been wanting to tell you all weekend;
in the car on the way here, but you'd made up a story
about a rabbit and a mole who were best friends
and it got more and more fantastic as we joined in
and laughed our way through the miles – the three of us.

I'd been wanting to tell you all weekend
and now here we are sitting in the late summer sun
outside your friend's house built around a tree in his wood,
the grass warm beneath us, constellations of daisies
swirling around dandelion suns, making our own galaxy.
The one I'm about to change.

I'd been wanting to tell you all weekend,
waiting for the right time in the motorway hum of bees
gathering pollen for their queen, who somewhere deep in her hive
is laying egg after egg in hexagonal cells, waiting as they hatch
into tiny white larvae that grow and grow, pushing out wing buds,
forming dark spots of eyes and in no time at all, it seems,
bursting out fully formed.

Mothering

The best way to acceptance is disguise
of the orphan or triplet lamb born spare;
this can conceive the bond that ties

two hearts together. Before the lamb can rise
the shepherd coats it with the mother's glair:
the best way to acceptance is disguise.

Get the timing right, the ewe won't realise
until too late, the stranger in the pair
and can believe the bond that ties.

Some skin the dead from neck to thighs
and give the foster lamb another's coat to wear:
the best way to acceptance is disguise.

The simplest acts can bring the most surprise,
in my hand, a small hand, resting there,
we both receive the bond that ties

and as good shepherds recognise
instinct mostly overcomes the doubts we bear.
The best way to acceptance is disguise
can this conceive the love that ties?

Fairy Tales and Step Monsters

Mirror mirror on the wall, who is the
motherest mother of them all?
Sabrina Orah Mark

Fairy Tales and Step Monsters

I wish I'd held your hand more often,
it would have been easy.
I wish I'd worried less

and made a nest of my fingers
for it to curl inside,
it used to slip into mine anyway.

Do you remember the models we made
out of cardboard and paper?
Rockets, market stalls

and castles from toilet rolls,
me holding things together
while the glue dried.

Did you ever look in a mirror
and long for three wishes?
However hard I tried I could only see

you through a window, hear your voice
on the other side of a door,
touch your arm through your sleeve.

Jesus and the Snorty Pigs

You had a magpie's eye for the religion they offered
at the church playgroup at the end of the road.
We said grace for a while until the excitement of chips
one day made you forget. You collected the little booklets
they gave out, and knew them from their covers;
Jesus and the poorly man, Jesus and the snorty pigs.

At Easter we didn't have a rock to heave away from a cave
so you hid behind the sofa and were born again
from a rolled-up rug, unwound with a flourish
on the living room floor. *Again, again* you shouted
until we drew the line at the tenth coming and settled
on a celebratory feast of squash and custard creams.

When we took you back that night
you bounced up the path and rang the bell but forgot
to put on your going home face as you shouted
Mum, Mum, I've been Jesus today and been borned again.
When she slammed the door, the flowers on the peony
dropped one after the other and lay purple at our feet.

The Year in the Castle

Each day we walked the road to the castle,
the path littered with the carcases of our failure.

When we drew nearer our heads hammered
with the force of her spell as we searched

the battlements and arrow slits
for a glimpse of your face.

We stood before gates of thick oak crossed
and bound with iron listening for your voice,

the keyhole was high above us and she kept the key
in the glass case of her heart all wrapped around with thorns.

Each day when we were turned away
we looked back

and sometimes could see you in a high turret
gold spinning from your hair.

The Year at Court

During that time driving through traffic lights
became a superstition. If they stayed on green
my one true wish would be granted, amber – nothing,
red – he would be banished from our sight.

My wish was always the same,
that the judge would send out
words like a spindle that would prick her finger,
words that would snip like silver scissors at her tongue,
words that would come threaded on the sharpest needle
and stitch her lips together.

And then there would be silence,
and the silence would break her spell.

I find myself driving faster towards junctions
fingers tightening on the wheel.

The Wish

The star fitted into her mouth. She tried to cough it out
but too late, for the star had run down her throat.

The Assistant Thunder God Chinese Folk Tale

It left a glinting trail of specks that embedded themselves in the softness of her gullet and she tasted the sparkle of them when she tried to speak. When it reached her stomach, the star surveyed the walls but would not be contained. It shone through into her liver, where it made a lattice work of her bile ducts and glazed them with illuminated facets like a shattered stained-glass window. Then on to her heart, where it pulsed around the chambers, hanging chandeliers in her atria and flaring searchlights through the doorways of her valves. It burnished her lungs with incandescent candles so each breath was a glistening vapour trail as it left the shimmer of her lips. She smelt the saltpetre and sulphur as the star blazoned its way through cracks in her skin leaving tinsel streams as it sped back to its galaxy saying no, I cannot grant your wish.

The Year in the Forest

Where were you that year?
Lost from us in the forest,
among giant oaks trousered with ivy
and dark pines that cast their needles on the ground.

We went in after you,
found clearings where you'd been playing,
where you'd left piles of stones and stick figures.
Once, we thought we glimpsed your red coat through the trees.

We searched for you,
on paths that twisted and narrowed,
became choked with brambles that snatched at our feet
while the king looked down from his castle and watched it all.

What could we do
but every week send you letters;
tiny white pebbles that shone in the moonlight,
to lead you back to us.

Waiting Room

Finding another person to love, is finding another person to lose.
                    To Throw Away Unopened Viv Albertine

We didn't know, the first time,
that you can ascend to Hell in a scratched grey box
that stinks of sweat and desperation.

We didn't realise, that first time,
it was possible to disappoint a room full of strangers
by just appearing in a doorway.

Hell has different disguises;
children's story books with the last page torn
out, jigsaw puzzles with pieces missing.

Hell likes surprises;
the magician's trick of vanishing
bodies and revolving doors.

And we had no idea, that first time,
that fear can curl around the memory
of cigarette smoke and trap it in the air.

Court Room

It's not excitement
that throws your heart against your ribs
when you hear your name called out,
or eagerness
that makes you rush to the opened door.

Slowed by the disarming thickness of carpet,
you hesitate to sit
on the spotless chairs arranged in tiers,
behind the microphones
straining on stalks for the opening cue.

All eyes turn
to the silent entrance
of the assistant
who directs our obedience
to the majesty of illusion
                and bids us stand.

Statements and evidence are shuffled
and placed face down on the table.
Did you follow those practised fingers?
Did you think you stood a chance?

You leave with a decision,
the deception of sophistry
and the thin strings of justice
attached to small hooks that jerk
you from there
                to here,
month to year.

The Year I Lost My Voice

I lay awake remembering what it was to have a voice,
to feel the vibration of air rise from my chest, resonate
in the arch of my throat and be made into a solid thing.

I moved my lips and tongue into familiar shapes and tried
out various possibilities, then tested the air in a long exhalation
but there was no resistance, just the moment of stepping off
a balcony
                before a fall.

A ghost of an owl slid past my window,
told me to search the hardest places.
So I searched
and at the top of a winding staircase,
found a room with four wooden boxes
and three silver keys.

I unlocked the first box and heard a voice that calmed
my pulse to the rhythm of his breathing.
The second contained a voice of hissed indignities
that scratched at my eyes.
From the third came a voice so mighty I fell on my knees before it,
the king said —

do not bother to search for the key to the last box,
the voice in there is of no importance.

The Court Decides

It wasn't thirteen fairies that sealed your fate
but a man in black robes, a king in his own little
castle and because those closest to you turned
on a spit of loss and hurt and jealousy.

Spite was the spindle that made you sleep
and the king so bored by his own omnipotence
looked over our heads when he gave the verdict
that closed you behind a screen of thorns.

We waited our hundred years; seeing a blond-haired
boy in every crowd, turning whenever a small voice
called out *Daddy* and tracing the scars of separation
with hesitant fingers when we undressed at night.

At the appointed hour we waited by the castle gates
wondering if your sleep had contained our dreams.
When the briars parted, we ran to you, woke you
with a kiss and held you as though you were glass.

Every other weekend

The judge said you could be a father every other weekend.
He didn't say what you could be on the days in between;
the days when you couldn't help small hands into mittens
or help brush tiny white teeth,
the days when you couldn't tidy away toys
or pick up socks from the bathroom floor,
the days when you looked in the mirror for two faces
and saw only one.

★

and two weeks in the summer holidays

We were allowed to pick you up at ten o'clock
but were never quite sure, until you were in the car,
that you were real.

Once we'd got past Doncaster and exclaimed
at the vast-bottomed, cooling towers,
clock hands started moving again.

One year we counted the black knots of crow's nests
along the A1 and laughed at the crowds of lawyers
and their flapping squabbles;

we laughed so hard our voices chased
them away over the fields.

The Father in the Weeks Between Seeing his Son

I feel the place in my chest
that you flew to when you were born,
that each day you hollow into a bigger hole
making a nest from the shreds of my flesh
and the weeks you're not here
leave a sucking vacancy that stops my breath.

Empty
is too small a word.

What I feel is a deep-sea abyss
where no sun goes,
just monster fish with unhinged jaws
who appear from nowhere and flinch
away when they see my eyes.
Or a labyrinth of tunnels
under miles of soil and rock,
that locks me in a silence so solid I can touch,
a darkness so real I can feel
it stroke the wetness on my cheeks.

So I go outside and sob at the moon
and it turns into a howl,
a raw and feral yowl,
that loosens atoms from my cells
and sends them streaming into the night
so bright
I was sure you would see them
as a meteor shower of sparks
arcing past your mother's window.

Statues

We've checked the bag for your toothbrush
and reading book, replaced newly washed clothes
but there's no script for this in-between bit:

the wait by the door; the pause in turning the page.
We try coaxing out some words, *two weeks isn't long...*

Finally, headlights in the lane prompt us to release
you. Running down the path you half turn to wave,
cast your spell, we remain as statues until you return.

Brothers Grimm

I read somewhere that originally
the Brothers Grimm made the mother
the evil figure in their stories.

Such was the outcry,
they invented the stepmother.

The truth is, neither of us was evil,
we both laid a trail of breadcrumbs
for you back to our doors.

Notes & Acknowledgements

CaCO$_3$ is an anagrammatic poem: the end of the line in each couplet is an anagram.

'The Thief' was commended in the Hippocrates Prize for Poetry in Medicine 2017.

'Chiropractic' was longlisted in the National Poetry Competition in 2018.

Acknowledgements are due to the editors of the following magazines where some of the poems have been published. *Acumen, Artemis, Atrium, Bare Fiction, Brittle Star, Butcher's Dog, Coast to Coast to Coast, Compass, Carillon, Curlew, Dodging the Rain, Fenland Journal, Magma, North, Poetry News, Poetry Salzburg Review, Prole, South Bank Magazine, Stand, StepAway Magazine, The Ogham Stone.*

Thanks also to Lindsay Fursland and Cambridge Stanza and Tim Love and Cambridge Writers whose thoughtful reading and insightful comments encouraged me to always try for a better version.